CONTENTS

What Teenage Drivers Don't Know

The Unwritten Rules of the Road
A Safety Guide for Parents and Teens

John Harmata
Paul Zientarski

Lake Effect
PUBLISHING

ISBN 978-0-9907570-3-0 Color Paperback
ISBN 978-0-9907570-4-7 eBook

Printed by:
Total Printing Systems
201 South Gregory Drive
Newton, Illinois 62448
(800) 465-5200
Fax: (618) 783-8407
www.tps1.com

Published November 2014

Library of Congress Control Number: 2014915968

Lake Effect Publishing, Inc.
2828 Hillcrest Circle
Naperville, IL 60564
(630) 301-8154
Info@unwrittenrulesoftheroad.com
www.unwrittenrulesoftheroad.com

DISCLAIMER: The material provided in this book is for educational purposes only and does not constitute legal advice. The *Unwritten Rules of the Road* are those rules that can only be learned from having had many years of driving experience. This book should be used as a compliment too, and in no way is meant to replace any States Rules of the Road or other mandatory tests necessary in order to obtain a drivers license.

PREFACE

John Harmata

In 1971 at the age of eighteen, I finally took and passed my driver's license exam. I was one of the last kids in my graduating class to get my license; I just never got around to it. But soon, having my license was critically important, because I had been selected to skate for the Chicago-based Midwest Pioneers of the International Roller Derby League, and I was about to hit the road. Over the next two years I would log nearly 300,000 miles and crossed the continent of North America five times.

I was raring to go, but woefully unprepared for the rigors of the road, including some extremely dangerous driving conditions and very long hours behind the wheel. Here's a taste of what lay ahead...

One afternoon, a teammate and I were on our way from Chicago to Green Bay, WI for a 7:00 p.m. game against the New Jersey Red Devils. We were expecting an easy 3 ½ - 4-hour drive under normal conditions. The roads were a little wet as we left Chicago, but we failed to realize, as we headed straight north, that the temperature began to drop quickly.

Coming around a long, winding turn on I-94 N, going only 55 mph, our vehicle started to swerve out of control. I tried everything I could to stop the slide: pumping the brakes, turning the wheels in the opposite direction... only to find ourselves in a 360°

spin, careening off the highway, across the median and multiple lanes of traffic. Finally, we ended up in a ditch facing south with a new appreciation for life and a healthy respect for the danger of black ice.

Fast-forward about twenty-eight years. As my children were approaching driving age, I began to teach them early about my *Unwritten Rules of the Road*: driving tips and techniques that are not emphasized or taught in Driver's Education class. By the time they were of age and ready to drive I knew, as a parent, that I had done everything possible to keep them safe on the roads.

After thirty-six years of working with teens on a daily basis and logging over a million miles behind the wheel I want to share what I have learned to help keep teens safe as they start to drive. Further, I want to help other parents have peace of mind, knowing they have done all they can to prepare their young drivers for whatever lies ahead.

FOREWORD

Paul Zientarski, BS, MS

As the Department Chairman for Driver Education at Naperville Central High School, in Naperville IL, I was constantly seeking ways to enhance our program. Adding new content to the subject and keeping it fresh can be an arduous task.

John Harmata, developed the idea of teaching students taking Driver Education, *The Unwritten Rules of the Road*: driving strategies that he had learned over many years.

As experienced drivers, adults often take for granted the simple lessons we have learned through our own driving experiences. Too often, we assume that everyone knows these common sense rules of the road. As a result we fail to teach them to our young and inexperienced drivers – the ones who need these lessons the most.

Mr. Harmata appears to have taken the art of skillful driving to a whole new level in teenage driver training.

What Teenage Drivers Don't Know: The Unwritten Rules of the Road will increase a teenager's ability to drive smarter and safer.

INTRODUCTION

One of the greatest privileges we have in America is the opportunity to acquire a driver's license. No matter what state you live in, every citizen has the opportunity to obtain a license to drive, and a duty to drive responsibly.

The objective of this book is to teach new and inexperienced teenage drivers how to develop safer driving habits, by increasing their ability to think and act responsibly while behind the wheel of an automobile.

What Teenage Drivers Don't Know: The Unwritten Rules of the Road is a great addition to state and independent driving programs.

Mayor A. George Pradel
Naperville, Illinois

ALARMING STATISTICS

According to the US Department of Transportation and Centers for Disease Control and Prevention, auto accidents are the leading cause of death for teens ages 15 to 20. Here are more shocking statistics concerning teenage drivers:

CELL PHONES AND TEXTING

- Drivers under the age of 20 make up the largest percentage of distracted drivers.
- Talking on a cell phone can double the likelihood of an accident and can slow a young driver's reaction time to that of a 70-year-old.
- 56% of teens admit to talking on cell phones while driving.
- 32.8% of high school students nationwide have texted or e-mailed while driving.
- 12% of distracted drivers involved in fatal car accidents were teens ages 15 to 19.
- 34% of teens age 16 and 17 admit that they send and respond to text messages while driving.
- 48% of kids ages 12 to 17 report being in a car when the driver was texting.

UNDERAGE DRINKING AND DRIVING

- About 1/4 of fatal teen car accidents involve underage drinking and driving (MADD).

- About 5.8% of 16- and 17-year olds and 15.1% of 18-to-20-year olds reported driving under the influence of alcohol in the past year (MADD).

- About 8.2% of high school students reported driving a car or other vehicle one or more times when they had been drinking alcohol.

- 13.5% of 12th graders reported driving after drinking.

- Kids who start drinking young are 7x more likely to be in an alcohol-related crash (MADD).

- 33% of the young drivers ages 15 to 20 who were killed in crashes had a BAC of .01 or higher and 28% had a BAC of .08 or higher (the legal limit for drivers over age 21).

- Nearly 60% of young drivers involved in fatal drinking and driving crashes didn't use a seat belt.

- 70 % of young drivers who died in underage drinking and driving accidents didn't use a seat belt.

- 27% of the young male drivers involved in fatal crashes had been drinking at the time of the crash, compared with 15% of the young female drivers involved in fatal crashes.

SOURCES

"Teen Distracted Driver Data" US Department of Transportation June 2011
"Teen Drivers: Fact Sheet" Centers for Disease Control and Prevention

COMMON DRIVING DISTRACTIONS

There are many distractions when driving, even if only for short periods of time. Some of the most common are:

Cell Phones - Teen drivers are four times more likely than adults to get into crashes while talking or texting on a cell phone. Texting while driving is the number one driving distraction reported by teen drivers.

Sending a Text Message - 46% of drivers under 18 have admitted to texting while driving. Statistics show texting while driving is as dangerous as driving after consuming 4 beers.

Music - Turning up the volume too high or frequently adjusting the media/changing stations. 61% admit to being distracted by their radio, CD player, or iPod while driving.

Food and Drink - 51% of people admit that eating or drinking had compromised their driving.

Slowing Down to Look at an Accident - 21% of drivers slow down to look at the scene of an accident. Commonly called "rubber necking," this behavior takes the driver's eyes off the road, impedes traffic, and risks causing a secondary collision.

Personal Grooming - 5% admit to combing their hair or applying make-up or perfume while driving.

Sleeping/Dozing - 5% admit to having fallen asleep or dozed off while behind the wheel. If you find yourself starting to nod off, pull over into a safe area for a short rest.

Arguments and Conversations - Never attempt driving following an argument with family members or friends. Even a seemingly harmless discussion with other passengers can distract a teen driver enough to diminish their reflexes. That is one reason teens should never be allowed to drive with other teens.

Pets - Don't let them loose inside your vehicle while driving. Dogs are good at jumping around the car and into your lap, and can interfere with your ability to reach the brake pedal.

Adjusting Climate and Blower Controls - Adjusting the climate controls takes the driver's eyes off the road and is just as dangerous as tinkering with the radio, CD player, or iPod while driving.

Navigation - Decide where you are going and lock in the route on your GPS while the vehicle is still in park. Never operate any type of electronic navigation devices while driving. For longer trips, study the map in advance and always have an alternate route ready in case of bad weather, traffic, or road closures.

DEFENSIVE DRIVING:
EXPECT THE UNEXPECTED

According to SafeMotorist.com, "Defensive Driving is essentially driving in a manner that utilizes safe driving strategies that enable motorists to address identified hazards in a predictable manner."

In general, teenagers underestimate or are unable to recognize hazardous driving conditions. Defensive Driving teaches students to improve their driving skills by reducing risks, anticipating dangerous situations, and making safe, well-informed decisions behind the wheel. These decisions require drivers to be mindful of the road and environmental conditions. They require 100% attention to the task of driving.

As a young, inexperienced driver you should get into the habit of "thinking while driving" rather than daydreaming or being distracted.

DEFENSIVE DRIVING STRATEGIES

At intersections, in parking lots, and even at 4-way stops, people are aggressive, impatient, and don't wait their turn. It's this negative energy that puts everyone on edge! Whether starting out from home or work, make a habit of completing this checklist:

- Check traffic and weather before you leave.

- Do a quick outside body of the vehicle and tire check before entering.

- Listen for unusual sounds each time after starting your vehicle.

- Check all mirrors and windows for clear vision.

Never assume anything! Always let the other driver commit first.

- When changing lanes, always clear the vehicle to your left or right. Never drive on another vehicle's blind side. You never know when the other driver may decide to change lanes.

- Watch for erratic drivers: speeding, weaving, or driving extremely slow, these are all signs of impaired driving.

To avoid being cut off by a vehicle changing lanes (*Fig. 3-1a*), always wait for all vehicles heading in your direction to pass before turning onto any street (*Fig. 3-1b*).

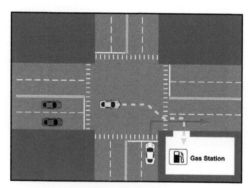

Figure 3-1a

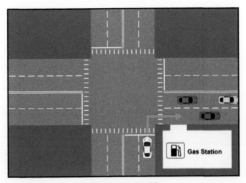

Figure 3-1b

INTERSECTIONS

If the vehicle to your left is extended beyond the line, partially blocking your turn: lining up your vehicle closer to the outside line (*Figs. 3-2a, 3-2b*) will allow you to make a safer turn into the lane next to them.

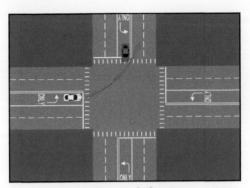

Figure 3-2a

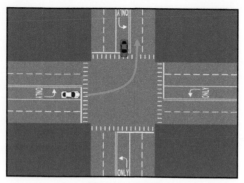

Figure 3-2b

Safety Tip - Never trust the turn signal of an approaching vehicle.

If you are in a double left turn lane waiting to turn left onto a multi-lane road, be patient and allow the other vehicle to commit first (*Figs. 3-3a, 3-3b*). This way you can avoid being cut off by the other driver if they accidentally turn into the wrong lane.

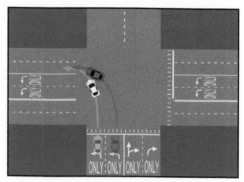

Figure 3-3a

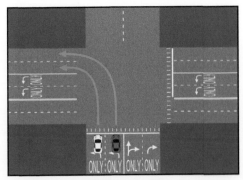

Figure 3-3b

When making either right or left turns at an intersection, never turn into the far lane. You may cut off another driver coming from the opposite direction turning into that lane (*Fig. 3-4*).

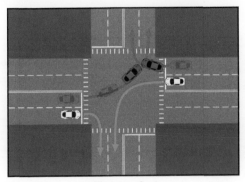

Figure 3-4

Morning and late afternoon rush hour are the worst times of day to fill your gas tank, for the following reasons:

- You can cause a traffic backup behind your vehicle when making a left turn into the gas station (*Fig. 3-5*).

- In bad weather, other vehicles may not see you exiting the gas station.

- If you do not make it across traffic, you can cause a backup through the intersection in the opposite direction.

11

An easier way to safely navigate in and out of the corner gas station is to proceed to and turn at the corner entering the station from a different direction (*Fig. 3-5*).

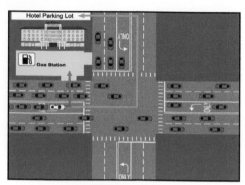

Figure 3-5

If traffic is backed up at this entry point too, continue down the street, turn back around, and proceed to the entrance of the gas station. By doing this you will prevent any gridlock or backup at the corner you just turned off of. It may take a bit longer, but traffic will continue to flow smoothly in all directions.

Turning across two or three lanes of traffic into a parking area during rush hour periods can be dangerous, particularly on a busy roadway close to an intersection (*Fig. 3-6*). You will not only back up traffic behind you through the intersection, but also run the risk of being blindsided.

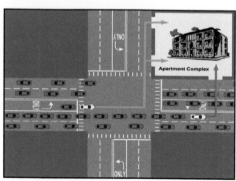

Figure 3-6

Reminder: Most intersection accidents occur when making a left turn.

ROAD HAZARDS

Predicting and preparing for possible road hazards is the responsibility of every driver. The following road hazards are common and could lead to accident or injuries that can be avoided if you remain alert and prepared in advance.

- Road Rage – always be aware of other drivers' behavior and actions. If you feel threatened with bodily harm, call 911 immediately.

- Paper bags or boxes in the roadway should be avoided as they may contain glass, nails, or other damaging materials.

- Dirt or gravel roads and parking in fields with high grass – these surfaces can be slippery, or hide obstacles or impediments that could be thrown by tires or puncture them.

- Downed railroad crossing gates – never zigzag through downed gates unless instructed by law enforcement.

- Stopping on railroad tracks – be sure you have enough clearance for your vehicle before proceeding across tracks.

- Potholes can be found almost anywhere at any time of year (*Fig. 3-7*).

Figure 3-7

VEHICLE HAZARDS

If any of the following mechanical failures occurs, please do not attempt to drive the car until it has been inspected by a qualified mechanic.

Breakdowns - If you believe your vehicle is about to break down, you should:

- Use your turn signal to indicate that you are pulling over.
- Turn your warning flashers on to alert other drivers that you are driving slowly or about to stop.
- Steer the vehicle onto the shoulder as soon as possible. Your vehicle should be completely off the roadway.
- Leave your hazard flashers on until help arrives.

Steering - If your power steering should fail follow these suggestions:

- Slow down.
- Grip the steering wheel firmly, applying more pressure than usual. Find a safe path through traffic to the side of the road. Move as far off the roadway as possible, and call for assistance.

Brake Failure - If your brakes fail, try the following steps until you can safely stop the vehicle:

- Pump the brake pedal hard and fast.
- Shift to a lower gear.
- Apply the parking brake slowly, so you don't skid.
- Rub your tires against the curb to slow your vehicle, or pull off the road into an open clearing.

Gas Pedal Sticks

- Shift into neutral (N) gear and find a way out of traffic – warn others by putting on your hazard lights.
- Apply brakes and pull off to side of road if possible.
- Turn off ignition.

Miscellaneous

- Hood flies up while driving – look through the crack between the hood and body of your car or out the side window.
- Wet brakes – test your brakes any time you've driven through deep water or a car wash, as they may pull to one side or not hold at all. Dry your brakes by driving slowly in low gear and applying them gently.
- Worn-out tires can lead to flats and bent rims (*Figs. 3-8, 3-9*).
- Blow outs - much more serious than a slow leaking tire. If you experience a blow out, quickly grip the steering wheel firmly and ease off the gas pedal. Do not use your brakes. When you feel your car is under control again, gently start braking and look for a safe place to pull over (*Fig. 3-10*).

Figure 3-8

Figure 3-9

Figure 3-10

WEATHER CONDITIONS

Adverse driving conditions are often caused by extreme weather. The ability to see clearly, stop efficiently, and maintain control of your vehicle is impaired by the weather. More in-depth guidance for how to manage severe weather is available in the Seasonal Driving chapter of this book.

Common weather related challenges include:

- Flooding (*Fig. 3-11*).
- Lightning strikes.
- Sudden wind gusts – (grip the steering wheel firmly to maintain control).
- Freezing rain - foundation for black ice (*Figs. 3-12, 3-13*).
- Heavy or freezing rains with accompanying high winds.
- Heavy snow – white-out conditions may develop (*Fig. 3-14*).
- Potholes - can be hidden from view during rain and snow-storms (*Fig. 3-15*). Do not brake if you hit a pothole: causing the car to lurch forward may damage the tire and/or rim. Reduce speed and drive your vehicle in such a way that it is centered over it.

Safety Tip - Properly inflated tires will help prevent flats caused by potholes.

Figure 3-11

Figure 3-12

Figure 3-13

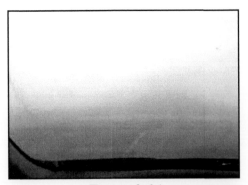

Figure 3-14

Figure 3-15

DRIVING ALONG COUNTRY ROADS

Paul D. Joyce

Driving along country roads is much different from driving on city streets because there are no center lines and drivers tend to stay more to the middle of the road rather than to the right. Not realizing that this works both ways, one day, I decided to open it up while ascending a hill. At the time, speed was of no concern, with few cars on the road and fewer sheriffs, my juvenile sense of immortality overcame my good judgment.

As I crested the hill, I immediately encountered an oncoming car, driving in the center of the road and directly in front of me. Terror quickly filled my mind. My automatic response was to brace for collision, slam on the breaks and turn out of the way. All this happened in a fraction of a second as the car began to skid for what seemed like eternity before leaving the road and running head-on into a tree.

Fortunately I walked away with barely a scratch on me. I had certainly dodged a bullet that day. Later I found out that based upon the length of the skid marks (110 feet) taken at the accident scene by the investigating officer, my estimated driving speed was around 100 mph. Needless to say, the Mustang I was driving was reduced to a Pinto by comparison.

I was lucky, the Mustang was sturdy, otherwise the incident would have resulted in an unnecessary teenage death, and my mother would have killed me.

COUNTRY ROAD HAZARDS

Country roads are not maintained as well as city streets and highways. They are poorly lit, poorly marked, and have little to no signage. As in the story related above, people tend to drive too fast and stay toward the center of the road. Country roads give the driver a sense of freedom and relaxation, but it is important to stay alert.

Country roads present different obstacles that you don't see driving in the city:

- Farm equipment and livestock crossing the road.
- Tractors driving slowly.
- Country stores and farm stands on the side of the road that entice drivers to slow down or stop suddenly.

Warning: If you have an accident in the countryside, you are likely to be far away from medical or police assistance.

BICYCLE SAFETY

Believe it or not, bicyclists have the same rights and responsibilities as motorists when it comes to using the roadways. Importantly, due to the size difference between a bike and a car, it is likely that a collision would result in serious injury for the cyclist. Therefore, special care should be taken when driving near cyclists or bicycle lanes.

- A bicycle is difficult to see when driving since they are much narrower than cars or motorcycles.

- Cyclists on the side of the roadway sometimes need to move more toward the center of the lane due to rough surfaces, debris, drainage grates, or other obstacles.

- Bicyclists may not pay proper attention to stoplights or stop signs, they also may not display hand signals to indicate turns or stops.

- Look for cyclists to be in any lane, travelling in either direction. It is your responsibility to yield to cyclists in crosswalks, sidewalks, and bike paths before executing a turn into a driveway, parking area, or side street (*Fig. 3-16*).

- Use extreme caution at night; bicyclists may not have the proper safety equipment, including reflectors and headlights, on their bicycles.

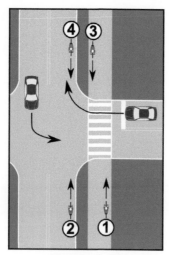

Figure 3-16

When passing a bicyclist, the minimum legal distance (clearance) to leave between your vehicle and the bicycle is three feet (*Fig. 3-17*). You must treat the bicycle as you would a slow-moving vehicle and stay behind it until you can safely pass.

Figure 3-17

A common mistake when passing a bicyclist is misjudging their speed. Turning right in front of their path (*Right Hook Fig. 3-18*) and cutting them off can be avoided by slowing your speed and waiting to turn behind them. The same can be said when making a left turn in front of an oncoming bicyclist – let them clear the intersection first before turning (*Left Cross Fig. 3-19*).

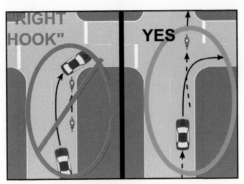

Figure 3-18

Figure 3-19

When turning off a road into a driveway or entrance you must yield when the bicyclist is in or near – the half of the road you are turning into (*Fig. 3-20*).

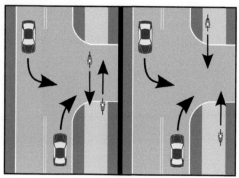

Figure 3-20

NOTES:

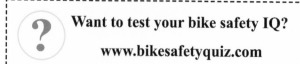

Want to test your bike safety IQ?

www.bikesafetyquiz.com

SURVIVAL STRATEGIES FOR HIGHWAY DRIVING

When driving on highways, you should be aware that a lack of mental alertness can cause what traffic safety experts refer to as "Velocitation". Velocitation occurs when a driver unconsciously begins to speed up without realizing it. Remember to regularly check your speedometer.

Warning: As a new driver, gauging distances can sometimes be a challenge. When wearing glasses or sunglasses, be sure you always clean them before driving. Dirty glasses can impair vision and depth perception of oncoming vehicles.

DAY DRIVING

Always keep a safe distance from the vehicle in front of you and watch out for other vehicles that may drift into your lane.

- On bad weather days, allow plenty of extra time getting to school or work.

- Never put makeup on or attempt to shave while driving.

- Never use a cell phone, and never, ever text while driving. Even hands-free talking on a cell phone is a big distraction and could cause you to miss your exit or possible hazards in the roadway.

NIGHT DRIVING

The most dangerous time to drive is at dusk. During twilight, the sky is still bright but at ground level it becomes progressively darker. The bright sky deceives the eyes and they don't adjust adequately. Make sure all lights, including headlights, taillights, and turn lights are working properly. Turn your lights on at the first signs of dusk.

Pssst... You may also want to consider night vision glasses.

Nighttime Driving Tips

- Check radio for news updates on traffic and weather conditions.

- Look away from oncoming headlights.

- Do not drive with bright lights on when there is oncoming traffic.

- Make sure of your destination - usual landmarks look very different at night.

- Never drive while drowsy or very tired.

- Watch for erratic driving behavior of others - avoid by slowing down or speeding up.

- Keep a safe distance behind the vehicle in front of you – one car length for every 10 mph.

Pssst... Do not wait for the brake lights of the vehicle in front of you to light up, warning you they are slowing or stopping. Think ahead and watch for a red glow underneath the vehicle in front of you. This will signify that the person two cars ahead of yours is slowing or preparing to stop and that the person in front of you will likely do the same.

26

Stay Alert - Stay alert at night by switching on the air conditioning, rolling down the windows, turning on the radio, singing, taking short stops, and walking around your vehicle. If you need to do any of these things…you should pull off the road.

ON AND OFF RAMPS

Upon entering the on ramp to a highway, gradually increase your speed until it closely matches the speed of the lane you will merge into. A gradual increase in speed will allow for better control of your vehicle and provide better grip as you round the curve and begin to enter the highway. Do not speed onto entry or exit ramps, as this may cause you to lose control of your vehicle and flip it.

Safety Tip - If you miss your exit, do not attempt to exit suddenly. Instead, go to the next exit, turn around, and come back.

TRUCKS, BUSES, AND SNOW PLOWS

When driving along the highway amongst trucks and buses, always pay attention to the following:

- Always give trucks, buses, and snow plows the right of way.

- Do not follow behind cement, gravel, or open-bed trucks. Loose stones or debris falling from a truck can puncture your radiator, crack a windshield, or cause a flat tire.

- Give yourself and the driver in the lane next to you plenty of space in case they have to swerve or change lanes quickly.

- Avoid side-by-side driving. When passing a truck or bus, do it quickly. A tired driver may start drifting into your lane without warning.

- Avoid driving in bunches. Drive in the least-congested lane. This will allow you time to react, to avoid accidents or lane closures.

- Listen for potential tire blow-outs – large vehicle tires will make a loud clapping sound before they blow out. If you hear this sound, pass quickly or back off to a safe distance.

Pssst... You can safely signal the driver of another vehicle you wish to pass by flashing your bright lights before doing so. In return, once you have passed, the driver of the other vehicle will signal back by flashing theirs, indicating that it is now clear to move in front of them. A courteous follow up gesture would be to once again flash your lights as a "thank you."

Warning: When following behind trucks, always watch for debris that may fall in the path of your driving. Don't slam on the brakes—you're not going to stop in time. Try and go around it by moving to another lane.

DEER IN THE HEADLIGHTS

Deer are most active during sunrise and sunset hours. September through November is mating season, the most active time of year for deer. When driving on roads near woods or open fields, slow down and keep an eye out for deer on the roadside. Often they can be found feeding on the shoulder or easements. If you see any deer, slow down. If there is one, there are likely to be several in the area. Keep a safe distance between vehicles and be prepared to stop immediately if necessary (*Fig. 4-1*).

Figure 4-1

MAP READING

Nowadays, map reading is becoming a lost art, but it is important to carry local and state maps in your vehicle and learn how to read them. Plan an alternative route to arrive at your destination in case of any road blockages or emergencies along the way. Never solely depend on GPS or navigational systems.

NOTES:

SEASONAL DRIVING: A TIME FOR CHANGE

When I was a teenager I drove through heavy rain and snow, blizzards, floods, and narrow mountain passes. One of my most frightful white-knuckle experiences was winding down through the Cascade mountain range in Washington State during a heavy rainstorm. From personal experience, most drivers, teen or adult, have no idea how treacherous a heavy rainstorm can be unless they have experienced one 10,000 feet up a mountain side with no guard rails to prevent the vehicle from going off a cliff.

Each season of the year presents different types of hazards for which you can prepare. Certain times of day are more dangerous than others. Knowing which hazards are likely to present themselves, and where and when you may encounter them, will allow you to prepare in advance so you can plan your drive time accordingly.

DRIVING THROUGH FOG

Fog (*Figs. 5-1, 5-2*) can appear at any time of the day or night: on city streets, country roads, highways, around rivers, and on bridges. It is only under extreme conditions that fog will last for several hours and cover a large area, sometimes for several miles.

Figure 5-1

Figure 5-2

Day or Night

- Use low beam lights when driving through fog.
- Be on the lookout for slowed, stopped, or parked vehicles on the roadway.
- Don't pass other vehicles unless absolutely necessary.
- Open windows slightly and listen for traffic that can't be seen.
- If fog is too dense for visibility, use the right edge of the road or center markings (*Fig. 5-3*), as a guide to keep your vehicle in the proper lane.

31

Figure 5-3

Safety Tip - If either headlight is not working, do not attempt to pass at night. The driver of the vehicle you are attempting to pass may change lanes unexpectedly, not realizing you are alongside them.

HEAVY RAIN AND LIGHTNING STORMS

A good habit before you drive is to tune the radio to a local news station for current traffic and weather conditions. If there are any trouble spots in your area, you will be able to avoid them by seeking an alternate route to your destination. You may also want to consider postponing your trip.

Three important things to remember when driving during heavy rains:

1. Do not use cruise control. Your vehicle may start to hydroplane and with the cruise control engaged, it may accelerate, increasing your chances of an accident.

2. When approaching a large puddle in the road, slow down and coast through it. This allows tires to grip the road much better. It will also prevent water from splashing up and impeding engine performance.

3. Watch out for standing water areas; if you cannot tell how deep the water is, do not attempt to drive through it. Deep water will drown the engine and you could be stranded. This is especially dangerous near rivers and in valleys where a flash flood might sweep you and your vehicle away.

SNOW AND ICE

There is nothing worse than being unprepared for winter driving. The following list of items should always be in your vehicle during winter months, especially if you plan on traveling more than 50 miles from home.

Check List

- Auto phone charger.
- Snow shovel, snow removal brush, and scraper.
- Driving gloves – grip control.
- Sunglasses.
- Windshield washer fluid – 1 gallon winter grade.
- Blanket and hand warmers.
- Energy bars and bottled water (enough for two days).
- Flashlight and extra batteries.
- Kitty litter – at least 20# - for wheel traction.
- Tire chains – if your state allows them.

Establish Clear Vision - It can't be stressed enough how important it is to **COMPLETELY**, not partially, clear all windows and mirrors of snow and ice (*Figs. 5-4, 5-5*). Full view around the entire vehicle will alert you to out-of-control oncoming traffic.

Figure 5-4

Figure 5-5

Always clear as much snow as possible off your vehicle's roof to prevent it from falling onto the front or back windshield while driving (*Figs. 5-6, 5-7*).

Figure 5-6

Figure 5-7

One way to keep your windows more resistant to snow and ice buildup is to treat them with one of the many aftermarket window treatments, and replace your wiper blades yearly.

Tire Check - It is especially important during the winter months to have properly inflated tires in order to prevent flat tires and/or bent tire rims (*Fig. 5-8*). Proper inflation improves gas mileage and tire grip to prevent sliding on wet or slippery pavement.

35

Figure 5-8

Black Ice - Black ice (*Fig.* 5-9) forms once the pavement's temperature drops below freezing and the air stays above freezing. This allows any type of moisture to freeze on the pavement. Even light rain or snow can become dangerous because as soon as it comes into contact with the pavement, it freezes. The ice forms a layer that's nearly transparent. Black ice can present itself at any time on any type of pavement and is unseen until it is too late. It is more common in the early-morning hours or at night.

Figure 5-9

Weather Conditions That Can Cause Black Ice

- Sudden high winds and temperature drop.
- Rain changing to freezing rain.

- Sleet freezing up on roadways.
- Shaded areas where the sun is blocked from warming the pavement.

Visible Warning Signs of Black Ice

- Slick driveways.
- Ice formation on power lines.
- Ice formation on trees.
- Ice formation on windshield wipers.

Reminder: Always use caution when crossing bridges, as the signs say "Bridges Freeze Before Road Surfaces." Avoid braking and lane changes while crossing bridges in winter months.

Blizzard Conditions - Blizzard conditions are most often encountered in wide-open spaces, e.g.: in the country or along highways (*Fig. 5-10*). Being caught in a blizzard while driving on the highway can be a terrifying experience; however, you can reach your destination safely by following driving guidelines for heavy snow:

Figure 5-10

1. Pull off the highway until roads have been salted. If you are caught between exits and cannot safely pull off the road, the key is to stay in your lane and on the road surface.

2. At a safe distance, follow in the tracks left behind by a semi-truck.

3. Use the centerlines as a guide (*Fig. 5-11*). You are more likely to stay safe if you can stay in your lane.

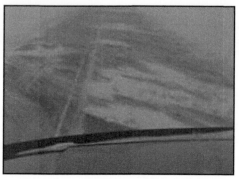

Figure 5-11

4. If alone on the highway, use the roadside markers as a guide (*Fig. 5-12*). They are located roughly 12 feet off the driving lanes to the right side of the road. If snow becomes too deep, find the nearest exit and seek shelter.

Figure 5-12

Should Your Wheels Ever Go Off the Road

- Take your foot off the gas pedal.
- Hold the wheel firmly and maintain a straight line.
- Brake lightly.
- Turn back onto the pavement sharply at low speed.

Pssst... It's snowing outside and you're going 25 mph. You can still get a speeding ticket for going 25 mph in a 35 mph zone. Why? Traffic, road, and weather conditions dictate the speed you should drive, regardless of the posted speed limit.

SUN GLARE

During the fall and winter months the sun rises later in the morning and travels lower across the sky. During the evening hours it will set sooner and can still present problems with vision and depth perception. One safe way to eliminate the morning and afternoon glare year round is by simply wearing a pair of quality sunglasses which incorporate the following key essentials:

- Polarized lenses to reduce glare and filter appropriate light levels (*Fig. 5-13*).
- Curved lenses to protect in front and to the sides.
- Thin temple eyeglass frames to maximize peripheral vision.

Figure 5-13

During the spring and summer months the sun will rise higher in the sky earlier in the morning, and is much brighter. On a clear day, morning and afternoon sun glare (*Fig.* 5-14) will slow traffic flow on both highways and major arterial roads and streets. Drivers heading east in the morning and west in the afternoon are most affected.

Figure 5-14

Warning: Using only a sun visor is not good enough, as you will tend to lose both depth perception and peripheral vision. As the sun rises higher in the sky or lower on the horizon, vision will eventually return to normal.

HOW TO BEAT EXTREME HEAT

Even on a pleasant 70-degree day, temperatures can reach as high as 85 degrees inside your vehicle. Never assume that the inside temperature will be the same as the outside. You must always be aware of the following:

Inside the Vehicle - Temperatures can reach as high as 130+ degrees in a parked vehicle during summer months.

- Never leave chocolate, cheese, ice cream, milk, or medicine in a vehicle for too long. Run errands early in the morning or late at night.
- Before entering your vehicle, open all doors and windows so heat can escape before entering.
- Place a windshield sun shade across back and front window areas.

Outside the Vehicle

- Never touch or place anything that can melt on the hood or roof of a hot vehicle.
- Never attempt to sit on a vehicle that has been in the sun.
- Park in a shaded area whenever possible.

PARKING LOTS

Navigating a busy parking lot on Saturday and Sunday or during the chaotic holiday shopping season can be challenging. To avoid anxiety, be tolerant of and defer to other drivers.

AWARENESS

Always note the location of disabled/handicapped parking areas, and restricted/reserved or permitted parking areas. To avoid paying fines: mind parking meters, time restrictions, and payment instructions.

Be polite to senior citizens who may not move as quickly as you. Allow them extra time pulling in/out of parking spots, and keep a safe distance as they walk across the parking lot and load their vehicles.

Also Keep in Mind

- Be aware of shoppers dropping packages.
- Don't park next to vehicles that restrict your vision when backing out; avoid parking next to trucks, vans, and other high-profile vehicles.
- When someone is backing up, stop and wave them on.
- Be alert to pedestrians walking out between parked cars.

BEHAVIOR

Always be courteous and proceed with caution in parking lots where children may be present.

- Never park in access or fire zones.
- Don't drive down parking aisles in the wrong direction.
- When driving in narrow aisles, stay to the center to reduce the risk of someone backing out into your vehicle.
- Never cut across aisles or park in a contrary direction.

Pssst... You can look below the undercarriage of a parked school bus or delivery truck to check if a pedestrian may be trying to cross in front of you.

CONDUCT

Be considerate of other vehicles. If you accidentally damage an unattended car, leave a note on the windshield with your name and phone number, date and time of the accident, and the license plate number of the car you were driving at the time. Use the Auto Accident Report Form (located at the back of this book) to record the make, model, license plate number, etc. of the other vehicle involved and report it to your insurance company as soon as possible. Without unnecessary delay, notify the nearest police department of the incident.

Reminder: Video monitors are everywhere these days. Do things right and avoid further legal consequences.

COMMON EVERYDAY HAZARDS

Parking lots, like roadways, present many hazards. Dings from shopping carts are commonplace, as are broken glass and trash in the roadway. Knowing what to look for will help you avoid such hazards.

Broken Glass

- Glass will appear to glisten on the pavement (*Fig. 6-1*). It may also be in noticeably large chunks. Drive around it if possible.

- Check tire treads regularly and remove foreign objects.

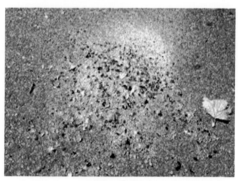

Figure 6-1

Shopping Carts

- When parking near a loose shopping cart, move it to a cart corral – the car you protect could be your own.

- When loading the trunk of your vehicle, align your shopping cart horizontally to your bumper to keep the driving lane clear.

Children

- Never leave small children unattended in a parked vehicle - heat stroke can set in very rapidly on hot summer days where the temperature inside a vehicle can reach up to 130+ degrees.

- Never leave a child unattended in a car that is running, even if you are only going to be a short while. Carjacking is a growing threat to both property and lives. In many states and municipalities you could be charged with child endangerment.

- Check behind your vehicle **BEFORE** you get in. Small children and pets are not easy to see from the driver's seat.

- Be extremely cautious when backing up; never assume that a parent will maintain control of their child.

Pets - Many pet owners consider their cats and dogs to be family members. Avoid leaving pets in unattended vehicles (*Fig. 6-2*), for the same reasons you wouldn't leave children. In addition:

- Pet theft may occur.

- A dog may destroy the interior of the vehicle in an attempt to free itself if it becomes anxious or hot in the vehicle.

- In older-model vehicles, a larger dog is capable of shifting the vehicle from park to drive.

Figure 6-2

Snow Mounds - During winter months, snow mounds (*Fig. 6-3*) up to 20 feet or more in height can be found in mall parking lots, making it impossible to see around them. Proceed with extreme caution when approaching the end of an aisle or before crossing or turning into another (*Fig. 6-4*).

Figure 6-3

Figure 6-4

DINGS, DENTS, AND DAMAGE CONTROL

Occasionally you may return to your vehicle after shopping to find it has some new scratches or dents on it. Responsible drivers take care to avoid causing damage to other parked vehicles.

Backing Out

- Don't turn wheels too soon when backing out.
- If your view is blocked, back out slowly and intermittently; if there is a passenger in the car, ask them to guide you out.

Extreme Wind

- Hold on to doors when opening and closing.
- Never leave a door wide open and unattended (*Fig. 6-5*).
- Watch out for runaway shopping carts.
- Keep windows rolled up to prevent foreign objects from blowing into your eyes.

Figure 6-5

Pulling Into Tight Spots - When pulling into tight parking spots, watch for obstacles: fixed objects such as signs and structural support beams of shopping cart corrals. If ever in doubt about pulling into a tight spot, just don't do it!

Pssst... Do not drive or park near a car that needs extensive bodywork - they literally have nothing to lose in case of an incident, and are likely to be underinsured.

NOTES:

WHAT TEENS SHOULD KNOW ABOUT AN AUTOMOBILE

This section provides a brief overview of some important features a teenager should learn about a motor vehicle before they begin to drive.

INSTRUMENTS AND CONTROLS

Gauges - The primary identifier of car trouble while driving.

- Engine temperature – indicates if the engine is running too hot. If so, pull over immediately and let it cool down.

- Tachometer - indicates engine speed in rpms - revolutions per minute. Driving with the engine running too fast causes excessive engine wear and poor fuel economy.

- Odometer – indicates the total mileage a vehicle has been driven.

- Trip odometer - can be used to calculate distance on each trip. It also may be used to record the distance traveled on each tank of fuel, making it very easy to accurately calculate the energy efficiency of the vehicle.

- Fuel Gauge - Always fill gas tank when fuel gauge reaches the ¼ mark, as sediment will settle to the bottom and can harm engines. Never wait for the low fuel warning light to come on. You may not make it to the next gas station before running out of gas.

Money-Saving Tip - Stretch your gas dollars even further by calculating your mileage. It is more cost- effective to spend a little extra at the pump in exchange for better gas mileage. Try different brands of gas, zeroing out the odometer after each fill-up. Use a calculator to figure your mileage each time.

CALCULATE YOUR GAS MILEAGE

To get your mpg, take the number of miles driven and divide it by the amount of gas purchased.

328 Miles Driven ÷ 14.538 gal. = 22.56 mpg

Warning Lights - Sometimes known as "idiot lights," these brightly colored illuminations on the dashboard are there for a reason. Knowing what they indicate can mean the difference between a major or minor repair.

Important: Seek Immediate Assistance - For the following items, have your vehicle serviced by a mechanic, and do not attempt to drive when these warning lights are illuminated:

- Check Engine – this light illuminates when the vehicle detects a fault with the engine management system. Could accompany immediate loss of power to the automobile and needs to be checked by a professional. If vehicle is operating under normal power, gas cap may be loose or pollution control censor may be faulty.

- ABS – this light indicates a fault in the ABS breaking system. Listen for a grinding sound when stepping on brake pedal, and have the brakes inspected.

- Temperature – warns of an overheated engine. Pull over immediately.

- Battery Warning - possible broken engine drive belt. Pull over immediately.

- Oil Pressure Warning – this light illuminates when the oil pressure sensor detects low oil pressure. The vehicle's engine should be switched off immediately to avoid severe engine damage.

- Air bag – these warning lights usually indicate if an airbag is disengaged – if the warning light illuminates unexpectedly, it could indicate a problem with the air bag system and may not inflate upon collision.

Attention Required - The following items are important warnings the driver can easily and quickly resolve most of the time. Some indicate that maintenance is needed soon, but the vehicle should be safe to drive in the interim.

- Tire Pressure – low air pressure in tires – possibly a slow leak; check and inflate as necessary.

- Door/trunk open – check that all doors and trunk are closed before driving.

- Low fuel – all vehicles will be different. As a rule, when this light comes on, assume you have no more than two gallons of gas left in the tank.

- MAIN REQD – change oil.

- Wipers – add washer fluid only; never use plain water.

DRIVING AND OPERATING

Safety Belts - Take some time and learn how to properly adjust both the lap belt and shoulder strap in your vehicle. Knowing this will make driving over long periods of time much more comfortable.

Lap-Shoulder Belts - When used, reduce the risk of fatal injury to front seat car occupants by 45% and the risk of moderate to critical injuries by 50% (NHTSA 2012*). Despite this, 15% of drivers admit driving without a seat belt. *Source: Traffic Safety Facts: 2011 Data Occupant Protection, NHTSA, April 2013, DOT HS 811 729 available at http://www-nrd.nhtsa.dot.gov/Pubs/811729.pdf

Brake and Gas Pedals - Use ease when stepping on the brake or gas pedal the first time you drive an unfamiliar vehicle. Some pedals will require very little pressure, while others require a slightly heavier touch.

Undercarriage Clearance - Reduce speed when traveling over a rough (bumpy) road and be cautious when approaching curbs, speed bumps or railroad crossings to avoid scraping the front bumper and undercarriage. The lower the clearance, the greater chance you have of damaging something under the vehicle. Avoid obstacles such as tree limbs and branches by safely maneuvering around them.

Changing a Flat Tire - Always carry a jack, spare tire, and wheel block (*Fig. 7-1*) in your vehicle at all times. Even if you don't know how to change a flat tire, someone else might. Practice changing a flat tire at home. To help prevent flats, make sure your tires are always properly inflated.

Figure 7-1

SERVICE AND MAINTENANCE

Check Fluids - Never use just plain water.

- Summer - use a washer fluid that helps clear windows of bugs and other hard-to-remove matter.
- Winter - use washer fluid with a freeze temperature of at least -25 degrees.
- Yearly - change antifreeze.
- Change oil and transmission fluids at recommended intervals.
- Check battery water level - make sure connections are clean, tight, and corrosion-free.

Tire Pressure

- Maintain proper air pressure at all times. Check monthly.
- Rotate tires every 5000 miles.

Wiper Blades - Need to be cleaned regularly to provide a clear view. Signs of wear include streaking, skipping across the windshield, and worn or split rubber.

Brakes - Signs of brake wear may include grinding, loud squealing noises, or difficulty stopping. If you experience any of these, seek repairs immediately.

Reminder: Look to the vehicle's owner's manual to learn more about required service and maintenance.

NOTES:

WHY TEENS SHOULD NEVER LET FRIENDS BORROW THEIR VEHICLE

An automobile is a valuable and powerful piece of machinery, the misuse of which comes with serious consequences for both the driver and the owner. Even if you trust your friends with your life, you should not trust them with your vehicle.

Six good reasons why you should never let anyone except family members borrow your vehicle:

1. **Accident Risk** - Teens are at the greatest risk of having an accident. In the case of a serious accident, the person to whom the vehicle is registered may be liable and could be charged with recklessness.

2. **Automated Red Light Violations** - Remember, a snapshot is taken of a vehicle's license plate. You may be responsible for paying the fine.

3. **Toll Violations** - The same rules apply here as they do for automated red light violations.

4. **Invalid Driver's License** - You never know when a friend may be driving with an invalid, suspended, or revoked license.

5. **Parking Tickets** - Whomever the vehicle is registered to is responsible for any and all parking tickets. Never assume a friend is going to admit to having received a parking ticket while using your vehicle. Left unpaid, these can add up to thousands of dollars in fines and possible license suspension.

6. **Under or Uninsured Motorist** - Never assume the insurance policy other drivers carry has the proper coverage.

Immediate family members are the only ones who should be using your vehicle. The only time someone else should use it is in case of emergency.

NOTES:

CRASH COURSE: WHAT TO DO IF YOU HAVE AN ACCIDENT

If you become involved in an accident, you should remain calm and immediately make a note of the other driver's license plate number, color, and make of vehicle. Write down the information or snap photos with your smart phone for documentation.

Reminder: It is helpful to keep a copy of an Auto Accident Report Form (found in the back of this book) in your glove box.

EMERGENCY PHONE NUMBERS

You should always carry the following emergency phone numbers in your wallet or glove compartment. In case of accident a first responder will have the necessary information to assist you and inform family members.

- Names and numbers of parents or legal guardian.
- Insurance company.
- Family doctor.
- Local fire and police.

DRIVER DEMEANOR

Body language can tell a lot about a person. Observe for signs that the driver of the other vehicle may be agitated – loud, obnoxious, etc.

- Observe the other person's speech patterns: slurred or disoriented.
- If the driver of the other vehicle is not forthcoming with information and abruptly leaves the scene, report it as a hit and run incident immediately to police and your insurance company.
- If the situation becomes aggressive, keep a safe distance from the other party and call 911.

INJURIES TO SELF OR OTHERS

Remain calm and check for personal injuries before attempting to move about. Call 911 immediately if possible, and provide the operator with your location and details of the accident. If you or anyone else in your vehicle appears injured and can't move, remain still until police and paramedics arrive.

When help arrives, do not attempt movement until you have been checked by the paramedics. The officer in charge will ask both you and the other driver involved about how the accident occurred. Tell him what happened in detail to the best of your ability.

ACCIDENTS INVOLVING VEHICLE DAMAGE

If you are involved in a fender bender without injuries, pull your vehicle to the side of the road as far as possible to avoid a secondary collision.

First Steps

- Remain calm.
- Call 911 immediately.

Do Not Say

- It's my fault (even if it is).
- My insurance will pay for everything.
- It's okay, I have full coverage.

While Still at the Scene

- Get as much information as possible.
- Take pictures of damage and the scene.
- When the police arrive, cooperate and tell them what you know.

After filling out a police report, call your insurance company to report the accident right away.

Reminder: Police may not become involved in parking lot or private property accidents because of private property laws. Always call your insurance company immediately to report accidents. In the case of bodily injury, call 911. Document as much information as possible about the incident, using the Auto Accident Report Form in the back of this book.

YOUR DAY IN COURT: WHAT TO EXPECT

By car insurance industry estimates, the average driver will file a claim for a collision about once every 17.9 years. So if you get your license at age 16, the odds are good that you will experience some kind of crash by the time you're 34. Over a typical driving lifetime, you will likely have a total of three to four accidents. **Source: Property Casualty Insurers Association of America, http://www.carinsurance. com/Articles/How-many-accidents.aspx*

Simply stated, "accidents happen," and knowing what to expect and how to act in a courtroom will help reduce the anxiety and stress of your first courtroom appearance.

YOUR RIGHT TO AN ATTORNEY

If the violation is severe enough to warrant legal counsel, you should consider seeking representation by an attorney. To find an attorney, start by contacting the local Bar Association referral service. They will provide you with limited free legal advice and provide names and contact information for a qualified attorney that can assist with your case.

Cases Warranting an Attorney

- DUI – not just alcohol – Xanax, Ambien, pain relievers - Zero tolerance under age 21.

- Illegal possession of any amount of cannabis or scheduled drugs (prescription).

- Underage consumption – possible driver's license suspension.

- Presence restriction – riding with others that have been drinking – everyone can be held accountable whether drinking or not.

- Use of an electronic communication device (cell phone) while driving is a felony when related to an accident involving bodily injury or death.

- Leaving the scene of an accident or failure to give information.

- Fake ID – possible driver's license suspension.

- School zone speeding violation - the critical issue with speeding in a school zone is that the offense does not allow court supervision. Any ticket for speeding in a school zone will result in conviction, which cannot be expunged from your driver's record.

- Failure to yield to emergency vehicles, or cause accidents or injury to public safety or service personnel at roadside emergency scenes.

Reminder: For any violation considered major, moderate, or that could result in jail time, you should consider legal counsel *(see Types of Traffic Violations below).*

DRESS CODE

Consider the image you would like to portray to the judge, jury, or prosecuting state's attorney. Whether you like it or not, your attire and appearance tells a story. Dress conservatively and be sure your hair is neatly groomed. Wear clothing that communicates you as a reasonable, honest, and serious person.

COURTROOM ETIQUETTE

While in the courtroom, be kind and courteous. When speaking, address the judge as "Your Honor" and address courtroom personnel formally using "sir" and "ma'am."

- Do not interrupt when being spoken to.
- No cell phones, gum chewing, or talking while in the courtroom.
- When your name is called out, raise your hand and say "here" or "present" clearly.

Reminder: Be sure to arrive early, follow instructions, and listen carefully. Do not assume anything; if you are confused, ask for clarification.

THE PLEA

When the judge calls you to approach the bench and asks for your plea, you have the right to:

- Plead guilty or not guilty.
- Request a continuance.
- Request an attorney (courts will appoint an attorney only for jailable offenses).
- Request to speak to the prosecutor.

Pssst... You have the right to discuss your case with the prosecutor. He will listen to any mitigating factors and he is the person you should plea bargain with, not the judge. The judge's job is to hand down the sentence if found guilty. If you are kind, apologetic, and show remorse when speaking to the prosecutor, he may decide to drop some or all charges against you.

TRAFFIC VIOLATIONS

Moving Violations - Breaches of state traffic laws, rules, or statutes that occur while a vehicle is in motion. Moving violations are divided up into three categories: major, moderate, and minor. Major violations should be considered serious traffic crimes that can be prosecuted through criminal courts.

Major

- Drinking and driving - DUI, DWI, or drug-related.
- Leaving the scene of an accident/hit-and-run (no injury).
- Hit-and-run (injury involved).
- Vehicular manslaughter/vehicular homicide.
- Driving without car insurance.
- Street racing.
- Excessive speeding (15 + over the limit).
- Speeding in a school zone.

Moderate

- Failure to yield.
- Texting while driving.
- Improper passing.
- Illegal U-turns.
- Improper signaling.
- Driving on the shoulder.

- Driving on the wrong side of the road.
- No proof of vehicle insurance.
- Minor accident.
- Speeding (10-15 mph over the limit).

Minor

- Seat belt violation.
- Littering.
- Rolling stop.
- Carpool lane violation.
- License restriction violation.
- Headlight/tail light violation.
- Disobeying traffic lights and signals.
- Failure to obey a traffic officer.
- Improper or illegal U-turns.
- Toll violations.
- Speeding (1-10 mph over the limit).

Non-Moving - Unlike moving violations, non-moving violations are any breach of traffic laws, rules, or statutes that are not tied to motion. Some common examples of minor non-moving violations are parking tickets, overly tinted windows, equipment violations (e.g. turn signal lights not working properly), and paperwork violations relating to insurance, registration, licensing, and inspection.

HOW GUILTY VERDICTS CAN AFFECT YOUR FUTURE

Most states operate a point system to track dangerous or careless drivers and promote safety on the road. A "guilty" verdict will result in points against your record.

Accumulating points on your driving record is costly. Your insurance premiums will go up, and after a specific number of points, your license can be suspended or revoked; to get your license reinstated you will pay hundreds of dollars in fines and fees.

Other Possible Consequences of Guilty Verdicts

- Driver's license revocation or suspension.
- Mandatory jail sentence.
- Vehicle insurance rate increases.
- Inability to gain key positions of employment.
- High risk rates for other important items like life insurance or bank loans.

Warning: Driving records are used for background checks, in court proceedings, and by insurance agencies to adjust your policy rates/premiums and investigate claims. A good driving record is a valuable asset and worthy of protection.

CONCLUSION

Concentration, patience, and control should be your guides when driving. Always be mindful of the power at your fingertips and the damage it can cause. In today's world, cars are getting safer, but there are more distractions than ever for drivers. Even if you are alert, the person in the car next to you could receive a text at any moment and carelessly drift in your lane.

When driving, you must focus 100% of your attention on the road and on the task of driving. In a split second, road conditions can change, and you must be prepared to react to protect yourself and others. Having the appropriate attitude when driving will enable you to focus more clearly, and ensure that you arrive at your destination safely.

No matter if you are new to driving or an experienced driver; you should take into account the *Unwritten Rules of the Road.* Helping reduce the number of accidents and fatalities on the roadways is everyone's responsibility.

"The Safest Driver in the World Is One Who Doesn't Drive."

~Anonymous

ACKNOWLEDGMENTS

We would like to extend our gratitude and appreciation to all of the following for having given their time in reviewing the material contained in this book. It is because of their expert opinions and commentary that we are better equipped to provide a more comprehensive book that will help to achieve our goal of teaching new and inexperienced teenage drivers how to develop safer driving habits.

City of Naperville, IL - Mayor A. George Pradel

City of Naperville, IL - Police Department

City of Naperville, IL - Michael DiSanto, City Prosecutor

Ed Barsotti, Executive Director - League of Illinois Bicyclists

Emily Koch Valencia, Contributing Editor

Paul D. Joyce, CPA State Examiner - Indiana State Board of Accounts

A special thank you is extended to Naperville Central High School students Faith Mellenthin, Jazz Tucker, and their art educator Amy Murphy for their time and effort in developing the front cover for this book.

ABOUT THE AUTHORS

JOHN HARMATA

John Harmata, business owner and entrepreneur, was born and raised in Chicago, Illinois. In 1978, John started his own business, servicing figure skaters from beginner up to national level competitors. In the fall of 2000, a member of US Figure Skating heard about his work and asked if he would be interested in contributing an article to *Skating* magazine. John has been writing the *Ask Mr. Edge* column for *US Figure Skating* magazine for more than ten years.

In May 2013, John published his first book, *Anatomy of a Figure Skating Injury,* which received a Global EBook Silver Medal award in the Non-Fiction Sports/Fitness/Recreation category.

His concern for child safety has been a priority in life. Raising two children together with his wife, John has experienced the concern parents have for their children as they take those first steps toward independence and begin to drive. John, creator and lead author believes that *What Teenage Drivers Don't Know: The Unwritten Rules of the Road* will help protect our most valuable possessions – our children's lives.

PAUL ZIENTARSKI, MS

Paul Zientarski has dedicated 40 years of his life to teaching students physical education, culminating his career as Department Chairman for Physical Education, Health, and Driver Education. As the Department Chairman for Driver Education, Paul's responsibilities included staff development, supervision, and film reviews for Simulator Systems, Inc.

Paul holds a BS in Physical Education and an MS in Communication Science, along with an Administrative Certificate. Paul is the Co-Director of DuPage County Institute for Physical Education, Health, and Driver Education.

Paul is an engaging speaker and has made presentations across the country on Learning Readiness PE, PE4LIFE philosophy, Childhood Obesity, Physical Education Curriculum, Technology use in Physical Education, Small-Sided Games, and Brain Breaks in the classroom. He has presented in 22 states to a variety of audiences, including the President's Council on Health, Fitness, and Nutrition in Washington DC.

Auto Accident Report Form

Accident Details

Day / Date / Time	
Weather / Road Conditions	
Location of Accident	
Accident Details	

Other Driver Information

Name	
Address	
Phone	
Vehicle Make / Model / Color	
License Plate #	
Driver's License Number	
Insurance Company / Phone	
Vehicle Owner's Name / Phone	

Damage Description

Your Vehicle	Other Vehicle

Passengers / Injuries

Collect the name of each passenger and describe all injuries

Your Vehicle:	
Other Vehicle:	

Witness Information

Name:		Name:	
Address:		Address:	
Phone:		Phone:	
Email:		Email:	

Photo Checklist

Use your camera phone to document the scene, personal injuries and vehicles involved and damage

☐	Other Vehicle (make / model / color)	☐	Property Damage
☐	License Plate of Other Vehicle	☐	Accident Scene (Wide Angle View)
☐	Damage to both Vehicles	☐	Road Hazards or Weather Conditions

Warning: do not photograph individuals or witnesses without permission as they may become offended and act aggressively.

Emergency Contact Information

Parents / Legal Guardian	Names: Home Phone: Mobile:
Vehicle Insurance:	Company Name: Phone:
Family Doctor:	Name: Phone:
Local Emergency Services:	Police: Fire:
Medical Alert: *Use this space to alert first responders of any medical conditions that may require special attention or treatment.*	